Vicious Recipes
Volume 6

Featuring Collaborative Efforts by:

Cyd Peterson
Dan Peterson
Patty Deas
Tami Keenan
Danielle Keopke
Connie Parish
Brenda Parish
Nona Taft
Victoria Taft
Brett Ockerman
Lynn Compton
Lexis Hamilton
Sara Nageotte
Jim Davis
Geoff Gunkler
Monica Reed

**Professionally proof read and edited by Tami Keenan,
CCR, BFD and SIS**

Author and proofing notes have been included and can be discerned thusly:
     Author notes: [smart ass remarks]

     Proofer notes: {dumb ass remarks}

Thanks again to our contributors, without you this would be a pitiful collection of my own recipes and you would all starve to death. So know that you are making the world a better place... to eat.

In this - the 6th edition of Vicious Recipes - we feature more submissions from outside the US - and several new submitters. Our friends and families are from all walks of life and we embrace each and every one.

Something else new for this year is [drumroll please] www.viciousrecipes.com.
Yeah... that's what I said, we're going to be on the interwebs! sorta... I own the domain and by the time you get your copy of this volume the first posting in my blog should be up and running.

You'll also see a barcode on the back cover, the book will be for sale on [another drum roll please] Amazon. It's my intent to attempt to cover some of the cost of production - we'll see how that goes.

Till next year... or till you read the blog... happy cooking!

Table of Contents

Drinks...

Burba Squirt

Put ice in a glass; fill halfway with bourbon and the rest with Squirt. Only drink 4 of these – or else!

Dan Peterson

Cyd's Starbucks magical latte

Cold: ½ Decaf/Quad/Iced Venti/Nonfat/One Splenda Latte
Hot: ½ Decaf/Triple/Venti/Nonfat/One Splenda Latte

Cyd Peterson

Raspberry Punch

Put one ½ gallon frozen raspberry sherbet in a punch bowl, pour one 46   oz can of pineapple juice and one liter bottle of ginger ale over the top.   The sherbet will melt/cool the punch – of course... you know... you can add a spiking agent, I'm just sayin...

Cyd Peterson

Jo's aka Mom's Green Christmas Eve Punch

Lime Koolaid prepared as directed (do they really still make that stuff)
Squirt
½ gallon of lime sherbet

Mix the first two together in a punch bowl to taste (who owns a punch bowl anyway?) Right before serving drop (gently or it will splash and make a big mess) spoonfuls of lime sherbet in the mixture.
She also used to make pretty ice molds to float in the punch.

Jo Cowles - submitted by Tami Keenan

Tic Tac

2 oz. Absolute Mandarin, 4 oz orange juice & 4oz Redbull over ice...enjoy

Jeni Peterson

Appetizers...

I Can has Cheeeez Ball?

Ingredients:

2 – 8 oz packages of crème cheeez – room temperature
One 8 ½ oz can of crushed drained pineapple
2 Tbsp minced onion
¼ cup minced green pepper
2 cups crushed pecans
1 Tbsp seasoned salt

Instructions:
Hold back 1 cup of nuts
Combine and mix all other ingredients – and really – the best way is to work it all together with your hands. Oughta think about washing them first. (or at least use that hand sanitizer stuff - unless you like living dangerously)
Form the mixture into a ball, spread the remaining crushed nuts out onto a plate and roll the ball – coating it completely.
Chill and serve with crackers and some sort of boozey drink.

Cyd Peterson

Sausage Balls

Ingredients:

½ lb bulk breakfast sausage

 [try the Albertsons store brand of hot sausage if you like it spicy {Can I use lunch sausage?} [I think breakfast is the best – I dunno you could check with Ruby]

1 ½ cups Bisquick

1 cup shredded cheese

¼ - ½ cup water

Instructions:

Mix everything together in one bowl. Roll into bite size balls and place them on a greased cookie sheet. Bake at 375 until brown.

Pig in = pig out… get it?

Cyd Peterson

Bean & sausage dip

1# Italian sausage, browned
1 med. onion, chopped
4 cloves garlic, minced
1/2 c. white wine
1 8oz pkg. cream cheese

Cook above ingredients until melted

Mix in:
6 oz. fresh spinach
1/4 tsp. thyme
1/4 tsp. oregano
1 can cannelloni beans

Put all ingredients in casserole dish

Top with:
1/2 c. mozzarella
1/2 C. Parmesan

Bake @ 350 for 40 minutes

Serve with sliced baguette or crackers

Karen Compton

Crustless Mini Quiches

I make a couple dozen of these at a time, then put them in containers and freeze them for a week's worth of lunches.

This recipe will be for one batch.

1 lb ground sausage (ground beef or turkey also works)
1 half of an onion, chopped
Peppers, chopped (I usually get a bag of mini peppers, then chop about 6-8 of them up)
12 eggs
1/3 cup sour cream
Cheese

Preheat oven to 350 degrees.
Cook the sausage. When it's about halfway cooked, toss in the onions and peppers. Once the sausage is fully cooked, take off of heat.
In a largish bowl, whip together the eggs and the sour cream.
I use my fancy Demarle medium cupcake pan to bake them in, but you can use a normal cupcake pan and spray it with cooking spray. {Good, cuz I don't know what a
Demarle cupcake pan is}
Fill each cake hole up about 1/2 - 2/3 of the way with the egg mixture.
Add a scoop of the sausage mixture.
Top with cheese!

Bake for 20 minutes.

Let cool and enjoy!

Danielle Keopke

Breakfast...

Sausage Muffins

1 Cup Bisquick
1 lb. cooked breakfast sausage
4 eggs, beaten and abused
1 Cup shredded cheese

Bake in a muffin pan , a muffin pan – 350 degrees – 20 minutes. Eat them while they're still warm.

Cyd Peterson

Good Old Fashioned Pancakes

Aron loves making these for the girls and we think they beat the shit out of Bisquick ones.

1 1/2 cups all-purpose flour
3 1/2 teaspoons baking powder
1 teaspoon salt
1 tablespoon white sugar
1 1/4 cups milk
1 egg
3 tablespoons butter, melted

Mix dry ingredients together first ant then add the milk, egg and butter.

Lexis Hamilton

Breakfast Pizza

INGREDIENTS
- 1 pkg. Crescent Rolls
- 1 (16 oz) pkg. Jimmy Dean Sausage - (regular, hot or maple)
- 1 c. Shredded Hash Browns - thawed
- 1 c. Shredded Cheese - Mexican Blend or your favorite cheese.
- 5 eggs
- ¼ c. milk
- ½ t. salt
- ½ t. pepper
- 2 T. Parmesan – grated

INSTRUCTIONS
1. Preheat oven to 375 degrees.
2. Take the Crescent Rolls out of the fridge 15 minutes before making.
3. Spray pizza pan or a sheet cake pan.
4. Brown the sausage in a skillet and drain.
5. Spread the rolls on prepared pan.
6. You will have to press and work the dough a little to make sure it covers the pan...pinch the pieces together.
7. Spoon sausage over the crust.
8. Spread the potatoes over the meat.
9. Spread the cheese over the potatoes.
10. Combine eggs, milk, salt, pepper, Parmesan together in a separate bowl.
11. Spoon the egg mixture evenly over the cheese.
12. (TO RECAP THE LAYERING: ROLLS, MEAT, POTATOES, CHEESE, EGG MIXTURE)
13. Bake at 375 degrees for 25-30 minutes.
14. ENJOY!!

Jeni Peterson

Salads...

Black Eye Pea Salad

2 Cans of Black Eye Peas, rinsed and drained
1 jar of Pimiento, finely diced. (Roasted red peppers are just as good.)
1 can of mushroom pieces, drained.
1 red pepper seeded and diced
1 yellow pepper seeded and diced
2 medium tomatoes seeded and diced
Small bunch of green onions (include a bit of green) thinly sliced
2 medium cucumbers peeled, seeded and diced
One small bottle of good Italian Dressing

Mix all ingredients and pour dressing. Stir again to mix and refrigerate
overnight.
Resist the instinct to salt and pepper until after tasting the next day.

Jim Davis

Spring Salad

Get a package of spring salad greens – preferably one with spinach [yes, spinach –
shaddup and try it]. Toss the greens lightly with Brianna's Blush Wine
Vinaigrette Dressing. This salad works best if it's served in a low flat baking type
of pan, cuz once the greens are dressed you sprinkle:

Blueberries
Cut Strawberries
Walnuts
Gorgonzola crumbles

And they all tend to settle at the bottom if you toss them along with the greens. I
stole this recipe from a Cookie Lee consultant in Phoenix and never looked back.
{Sounds like dessert salad to me}
Cyd Peterson

Junk

Old family recipe revealed for the Junk that it is:

Three ingredients, folks.

Big box of Lime Jello
16 oz can of crushed pineapple, drained very well
8 oz package of cream cheese, the softer the better

Fix the Jello like you normally would, reserve a little in a separate bowl. While it's setting up or chillin' as someone would say, mash the cream cheese in the separate bowl of reserved Jello till it's creamy and consists of little, tiny chunks of cream cheese. When the Jello is pretty much set, mix in the creamed cheese and pineapple; chill until ready to slurp it up. Viola, easy-peasy, you have just made the infamous Junk {or cream cheese salad – that's what it says on the recipe card I found in Mom's old recipe box written in her handwriting}

Tami Keenan

Main Courses...

Chicken Avocado Burritos

2 cups cooked and shredded chicken (or 2 chicken breasts, salt and pepper- to taste, 1 Tablespoon mustard, 1 Tablespoon olive oil)
1 cup grated cheese (I use mozzarella)
1 avocado -diced
 2 Tablespoons cilantro-chopped
4 large tortillas
 4 Tablespoon sour cream
1 Tablespoon oil

Instructions
1.   Heat 1 tablespoon olive oil in a frying pan, place chicken breast sprinkled with salt and pepper and roast for about 5 minutes on each side. Spread 1 tablespoon mustard over the chicken, add about ¼ cup water add cook covered for a few more minutes.
2.   Cut cooked chicken into thin stings.
3.   Mix the chicken, cheese, cilantro, and the diced avocados.
4.   Spread 1 tablespoon sour cream on each tortilla, add ¼ of the mixture, form a roll.
5.   Heat 1 tablespoon oil into a pan and place all four tortillas on the pan, cook for 2 minutes on medium- high heat. Flip on the other side and cook for another minutes or until the the tortillas are golden

 Karen Compton

Slow cooker Salisbury Steak

2 pounds lean ground beef
1 envelope dry onion soup mix
1/2 cup Italian seasoned bread crumbs (panko)
1/4 cup milk
1/4 cup all-purpose flour

2 tablespoons vegetable oil
2 cans condensed cream of mushroom soup
1 packet dry au jus mix (or beef gravy mix)
3/4 cup water
In a large bowl, mix together the ground beef, onion soup mix, bread crumbs, and milk using your hands. Make 8 patties.
Heat the oil in a large skillet over medium-high heat. Dredge the patties in flour just to coat, and brown on both sides in the hot skillet. Place browned patties into the slow cooker stacking alternately like a pyramid. In a medium bowl, mix together the cream of mushroom soup, au jus mix, and water. Pour over the meat. Cook on the Low setting for 4 or 5 hours, until ground beef is well done.

Nona Taft

Spaghetti Sauce

Ingredients:
Ground Beef and/or ground hot Italian Sausage
Johnsonville Hot Italian Sausage links
Chopped onion
Chopped yellow and/or red peppers
Small can of sliced black olives
Small bottle of salad or sliced green olives
Several cans of tomato sauce
Several cans of diced tomatoes
One large can of Hunts Traditional or Italian Sausage Spaghetti Sauce
A coupe cans of tomato paste
Salt
Instructions:
The specific measurements are not listed because it's done on a sliding scale, the bigger the pot – the more ingredients!
Start by browning the ground beef or Italian sausage, once it's fully cooked, drain excess grease. Add in the chopped onion and peppers; decide for yourself if you want the onions and peppers chopped large or small.
When the onions start to appear clear start adding the canned tomato products, start with the spaghetti sauce and then add in the plain tomato sauce and diced tomatoes, it's about 50/50 for each. Stir thoroughly and then add tomato paste, this is your only thickening agent – so don't skimp.
Add olives and salt to taste. Cook for about an hour (less would prolly work if you're in a hurry). But don't overcook.
Now cook the pasta, smear it with sauce and put it in your belly. {The proofer declines to change anything in this recipe, because I've had it more than once and you can't change perfect spaghetti sauce}

Cyd Peterson

Lasagna

Ingredients:
One box of barilla no boil lasagna noodles, uncooked
2 eggs
1 15 oz container of ricotta cheese
4 cups shredded mozzarella cheese
½ cup grated Parmesan cheese
Several cups of leftover spaghetti sauce
Prep:
Preheat oven to 375, beat eggs, stir in ricotta and ½ of the mozzarella cheese (maybe in a bowl instead of the oven)
Assemble:
Use an oiled 13 x 9 baking pan (I usually use a bigger roasting pan and about double the ingredients)
Cover the bottom of the pan with sauce, layer lasagna sheets, 1/3 of the ricotta mixture 1/3 of the remaining mozzarella and cover with sauce. Repeat, I usually do 3 layers. On the top layer, add the remaining mozzarella.
Cook:
Bake covered with foil for about 50 – 60 minutes, uncover and bake till the cheese is bubbly and melted. Let it stand at least 15 minutes before cutting.

Cyd Peterson

Short Rib Pasta Sauce

1 tbs olive oil
short ribs (I used one package maybe 1 1/2 lb) brown in oil 3-4 minutes
per side, remove from pot that can go into oven
1 red onion chopped brown in pot
4 oz pancetta brown in pot with onion 3-4 minutes
3 cloves garlic minced brown with above 1 minute
add to pot:
1 cup red wine
2 c tomato puree
4 cups beef broth
browned short ribs

We love this served over capellini or tagliatelle pasta

Karen Compton

Garlic baked chicken breasts

4 boneless & skinless chicken breasts
4 tablespoons brown sugar
4 garlic cloves, minced
3 teaspoons olive oil

Set the oven to 500 degrees. Fry garlic with oil until it becomes soft.
Put the garlic in brown sugar. Put the chicken in a dish for baking. Put
the garlic on the chicken. Combine salt and/or pepper as you like.
Bake without cover for approx 20 mins.

Nona Taft

Chicken Cordon Bleu Casserole

Base:
1 large rotisserie chicken, meat removed and pulled (about 5-6 C)
1/2 pound sliced deli-style black forest ham, chopped
1/2 pound sliced swiss cheese
Sauce:
4 Tb butter
4 Tb flour
3 C milk
2 Tb lemon juice
1 Tb Dijon mustard
1 1/2 tsp salt
1/2 tsp smoked paprika
1/2 tsp pepper
Topping:
4 Tb melted butter
1 1/4 C seasoned bread crumbs
1/4 C Parmesan cheese

1. Preheat oven to 350 degrees and spray a 9×13 casserole dish with nonstick spray. Layer the chicken in the bottom of the dish followed by the ham and finally the swiss cheese.

2. In a medium saucepan, melt the butter over medium heat. Whisk in the flour and cook for 1 minute. Slowly add the milk, whisking to keep clumps from forming. Turn the heat to high and cook until the sauce thickens and boils completely, whisking often. Remove from the heat and add the remaining sauce ingredients. Pour the finished sauce over the base layer already in the dish.

3. In a small bowl, mix together the topping ingredients until the butter is evenly distributed over the crumbs. Sprinkle over the top of the dish and bake for 45 minutes. Allow to cool for 10 minutes before serving so the sauce will thicken just a bit.

Jeni Peterson

Enchilada Pie

A Mexican version of Lasagna. So when making this dish, picture making lasagna with tortillas instead of noodles; chicken instead of meat; and with more ingredients. ENJOY!!!!
Ingredients:
1 pack of tortillas
2 cans of enchilada sauce
Lots of shredded cheese!
2 cans of sliced olives
2 pieces of chicken breast
Preheat oven to 350 degrees
In a casserole dish, layer the bottom with enchilada sauce. Use just enough to cover the bottom. Do not use the whole can, silly.
Add a layer of tortillas (1-3 pieces, depending on size of dish)
Add a layer of other ingredients. Feel free to use as much or as little as you like.
Pour some more sauce over the ingredients.
Repeat adding layers until you are out of room. (in the pan, that is)
Finish the dish with a tortilla layer, sauce and cheese.
Bake for 20-30 minutes
TA DA!!! You can add or take away any ingredient as you like.

Jeni Peterson

Easy Shredded Chicken

Boil your chicken boobs. If you have large boobs, cut them in half. [how will this help cook the chicken?
Once your boobs are boiled, [now i gotta boil my boobs too?] put them in your Kitchen-aid Blender with your paddle attachment on. [what if i don't have one?]
Start the blender at a low speed, then raise it a couple of times until the boobs are shredded to your liking.

Danielle Keopke

Tamale Pie

Ingredients:
2 lbs ground beef
2 packages of Jiffy corn muffin mix
2 cups cold water
1 can of black or pinto beans
1 cup of shredded cheddar cheese
1 jar of salsa – you choose

Instructions:
Preheat oven to 425
Cook ground beef, feel free to add onion and/or any spices you might like – possibly taco seasoning. (how about some cumin, so you can finally use up that jar of it languishing in the cupboard) Once cooked, add beans, here again feel free to add other ingredients, possibly green chili peppers or green onions (if your name is now or ever has been Peterson, you'll no doubt want to add black olives), etc.
Combine muffin mix with water and pour into an oiled 9 x 13 baking pan. Spoon meat and bean mixture into the batter, try to get it spread evenly – who wants a bite with no meat? (a vegan maybe)
Bake for 30 minutes or so, check to see if it springs back when touched or it starts to pull away from the edge of the pan. Remove from oven, sprinkle with cheese and let it stand for 5 minutes before serving.
Cut into sections and serve with salsa on top – shredded lettuce is also awesome on top! Beer is optional for some – required for others.

Cyd Peterson

Southwestern Chicken & Rice

Ingredients:
4 boneless skinless chicken breast halves
1 cup salsa
2 cups water
2 cups Minute Rice, uncooked
1 can black beans
1 cup shredded cheddar cheese

Instructions:
Bring chicken, salsa and water to boil in a large skillet, cover and let simmer for 10 minutes. Turn up the heat and bring it to a boil again, stir in rice and beans. Sprinkle cheese over the top and cover. Cook on low for 5 minutes and POOF – it's done!

Cyd Peterson

Spicy Parmesan Chicken Boobies

Ingredients:
½ cup grated Parmesan cheese
¼ cup Italian bread crumbs
1 tsp each; oregano and parsley flakes
¼ tsp each; paprika, salt and pepper
2 boneless skinless chicken breast halves
2 tbsp butter or margarine, melted

Instructions:
Mix cheese, crumbs and seasoning. Dip chicken in butter, coat with cheese mixture. Put them in an oiled baked pan and bake for 20 – 25 minutes at 400 – until cooked through, unless you're stupid and like salmonella for dessert.

Cyd Peterson

Ravioli Bake

Ingredients:
1 bag mini cheese ravioli rounds
2 jars spaghetti sauce
1 lb beef
1 lb pork sausage
2 cups shredded mozzarella cheese
2 cups shredded Monterey Jack cheese
Brown beef and pork together in large pan. Drain. Put back in pan and add ravioli and spaghetti sauce, warm through. Pour mixture into 9x13 pan, top with cheeses. Bake, covered with aluminum foil, for 30 min at 450 degrees.

Brenda Parish

Scotty's Special (a.k.a. Amy's Special)

Cook a pound of hamburger and make sure to season it the way you like it.
Add like 4-5 eggs and cook like you were making scrambled eggs.
Add salt and pepper, cheese, ketchup or serve over bread if you would like.
All done!

Danielle Keopke

Meat Loaf

2 pounds ground beef
½ cup Italian bread crumbs
10 saltines – crushed pretty fine
A cup of finely chopped onion
2 teaspoons of Montreal Steak Seasoning
3 eggs
Catsup

Mix all ingredients except for the catsup, very, very thoroughly and free form the mixture into an object that looks like a loaf onto a 9 x 13 pan. Squeeze some catsup over the top in a zig zag pattern. Bake at 350 for about an hour/hour and 20 or 30.

I like meat loaf to have a very consistent and smooth texture, it's easier to slice and much easier to make sandwiches the next day. Some people (Dan) like gravy – I say sacrilege! Serve with catsup!

Cyd Peterson

Meatloaf

1 lb ground beef
1/2 Cup plain dry breadcrumbs
1 egg
Garlic Powder to taste
Dash Worcestershire sauce
1/3 cup ketchup (organic makes a big taste difference, I recommend it!)
1/4 cup packed golden brown sugar
1/4 cup apricot-pineapple preserves
Ground pepper to taste

Preheat oven to 350*
In large bowl mix meat, egg, bread crumbs, garlic powder, and Worcestershire.
Bake for 30-50 minutes (I've always done 40, and it's been perfect, but ovens vary)

In separate bowl mix ketchup, preserves, brown sugar, and ground pepper to taste.
Pour over meat 20 minutes before removing from oven.

I've always done a total of 60 minutes, but I like my meat a little well done. Enjoy!

Monica Reed

Tamwich – that's right, not Manwich

Most of my recipes are not made with measurements, just throwing in some of this and that. And green peppers don't like us so we always use yellow peppers in the Keenan house. I came up with this one rainy Saturday when I was hungry.

Here's the ingredients:
1 ½ lb. ground beef
1 large onion chopped
1 yellow pepper chopped
2 tbsp butter
1 medium can of Bush's baked beans – original recipe
Small can of diced tomatoes
Barbecue sauce
Ketchup
Mustard
Mrs. Dash table blend
Salt
Pepper
Seasoning salt
Garlic powder

I brown the ground beef till it's almost done, drain and rinse it, put it back in the frying pan with the onion and yellow pepper I've chopped and sautéed in butter while the meat is browning. I let that cook together a while, then I add the tomatoes, baked beans (not drained) and all the condiments and seasonings. I used probably ¼ cup of barbecue sauce and ketchup and maybe 2 tbsps mustard, and the seasonings to taste. Then I throw it all in the Crockpot and let it simmer till we're ready to eat it. Usually easier to take a bite of Tamwich and then a bite of roll or bread cuz it's pretty sloppy, but oooh, is it good!

Tami Keenan

Hawaiian Pineapple Pork Chops

10 big fat pork chops
12 oz ketchup
1 ½ cups water
½ cup sugar
½ cup vinegar
Salt and pepper
Small can crushed pineapple

Brown the chops slowly in a greased pan just to a light golden brown remove and transfer to an oven pan. Arrange them in a single layer. In a saucepan mix the rest of the stuff 'cepting the pineapple and bring to a boil, and cook to thicken. Pour the sauce over the chops and top with the pineapple, juice too. Cover and bake at 275 for 2 to 3 hours.

Nona Taft

Western Mac

Ingredients:
1 box Kraft mac and cheese
1 lb ground beef
1 12 oz can of tomato paste
1 can corn
4 oz shredded cheese (1/2 of a regular size bag)

Instructions:
Brown the ground beef and mix with all the other ingredients. Pour into a small oiled casserole pan. Bake at 350 till cheese is all melted/melty.

Dan Peterson

Chicken Alfredo Roll-ups

9 lasagna noodles
2 ½ cups Alfredo sauce (recipe following)
2 cups cooked, shredded chicken
Oregano
Garlic salt
3 cups shredded Mozzarella, or cheese of your choice

Word to the wise. Give yourself plenty of time to prepare things one at a time. It can get very overwhelming if you try to cook the chicken, noodles, and Alfredo sauce at the same time.

First, cook and cut the chicken. (you could cut and cook the chicken – it won't hurt the final version)

Boil 8-10 cups water in a large pan, then cook lasagna noodles until al dente (that means tender, but still firm). Cook 1 or 2 extra just in case any lasagna noodles break while stirring them. Drain and rinse the noodles with cold water to prevent them from sticking to each other. Then, lay out each noodle individually and blot dry with a paper towel.

This is where I normally preheat the oven to 350.

*If you are making the Alfredo sauce, continue. If not, skip this part.

The Best Garlic Alfredo Sauce

½ cup butter
2 ounces cream cheese
2 cups heavy cream (or substitute half and half)
2 teaspoon garlic powder
½ tsp. fresh minced garlic
Salt and freshly ground black pepper
½ tsp. dried oregano
⅔ cup Parmesan cheese

25

In a medium to large saucepan melt the butter over medium heat.
Add fresh minced garlic and cook for 1 minute, or until fragrant.
Add the cream cheese and whisk to smooth and melted.
Whisk in the heavy cream.
Season with the garlic powder, salt and pepper.
Bring to a simmer and whisk frequently until sauce thickens, around 15 minutes.
Stir in the cheese and when melted, remove from heat and serve.

Makes 2 ½ cups

Spray an 8x8 pan with non-stick spray and pour ½ cup Alfredo sauce, or just enough to cover the bottom of the pan.

Spread about 2 tbs. Alfredo sauce over each noodle. (If there is too much sauce you will have a big mess on your hands!)
Sprinkle oregano and garlic salt on top of sauce.
Take 1/9ish of the shredded chicken and spread it out evenly over each noodle.
Add approx. 3 tbs. cheese.
Now Roll Up! Start at one end and roll the noodle over the toppings.
You will need to lift the noodle a little to prevent squishing out the inside ingredients while rolling.
Place the roll-ups in the pan, one by one, seam-side down so they don't come undone.
Once they are all in the pan, pour the remaining Alfredo sauce over the top.
Top with remaining cheese.
Bake for about 30 minutes, or until the cheese is completely melted on top.

Serves 3, 3 roll-ups each

Daniel Keopke

Spicy Parmesan Chicken Boobies

Ingredients:
½ cup grated Parmesan cheese
¼ cup Italian bread crumbs
1 tsp each; oregano and parsley flakes
¼ tsp each; paprika, salt and pepper
2 boneless skinless chicken breast halves
2 tbsp butter or margarine, melted

Instructions:
Mix cheese, crumbs and seasoning. Dip chicken in butter, coat with cheese mixture. Put them in an oiled baked pan and bake for 20 – 25 minutes at 400 – until cooked through, unless you're stupid and like salmonella for dessert.

Cyd Peterson

My best Tofu recipe yet

Grab your tofu
Throw it in the trash
Go get a steak
Cook it on the grill

Cyd Peterson

Lazy Chicken Bake

Ingredients:

1 1/2 pounds large Yukon gold potatoes, cut into 1 1/2-inch pieces
4 cloves garlic, smashed and coarsely chopped
2 tablespoons extra-virgin olive oil
Kosher salt
1 1/2 pounds skinless, boneless chicken thighs
Paprika
Freshly ground pepper
Cayenne Pepper
1 lemon
2 large or 3 medium red onions, halved and thinly sliced
Directions
Preheat to 375 degrees F. Put the potatoes, garlic, olive oil, 1 tablespoon water and 1/2 teaspoon salt in a large bowl and toss to coat. Lay potatoes out on a baking sheet with edges or in a Pyrex-style baking dish.
Pat the chicken dry and cut into pieces or leave whole. Sprinkle with the paprika, salt, pepper, and a dash of cayenne (to taste). Add lemon juice or wedges. Toss together and place on top of potatoes. Chop and scatter the onions on top.
Roast for approximately 20-25 minutes if potatoes were cut, or 45-50 if not cut. You can add a bit of water to the bottom occasionally, to ensure that nothing gets dried out.
Pull it out and serve.

Lexis Hamilton

Beef Stroganoff

Find some wonderful deal on a couple lbs of cheap steak {you cheapskate!} Slice it into small strips, rather like julienne.

In a large(ish) plastic bag combine flour and seasonings – I just use Montreal Steak Seasoning.

Put the meat into the bag and coat it all evenly with the flour mixture.

Heat a large sauté pan, add oil and brown the meat strips. {are we back to the brown in a sauté pan again?}

Mix a cup of water with some beef base (or bouillon).

Empty a 16 oz container of sour cream on top of the still sizzling beef – add about 1/2 cup of the water/beef base mixture and stir until it blends well and coats all the meat. Add more juice to make it as creamy as you like.

And BAM – that shit is done.

Best served over a nice thick egg noodle, Trader Joe's has a great version, the taste and texture resembles homemade. You can use rice if you prefer.

Cyd Peterson

Tater Tot Casserole

1 lb ground beef
1 can of cream of mushroom
1 bag of tater tots
Black Olives {is she a Peterson?} [she is!]

Cheese

Preheat oven to 350

Smooth uncooked ground beef evenly into bottom of a casserole dish
Spread cream of mushroom over the meat
Optional Sprinkle olives on top of soup
Pour out bag of tater tots on top
Optional Cover with shredded cheese
Bake for 1 hour

Danielle Keopke

29

Grandma's Meatballs

Preheat oven to 350

2 lbs. lean ground beef
1 can condensed chicken & rice soup
2 T. chopped onion
1 sleeve of crushed saltine crackers
1 egg
1 ½ tsp. salt
¼ tsp. pepper
2 cans cream of mushroom soup
1 ½ cans water
1 cup oil
Cornflake crumbs

Heat oil in electric skillet. Put some cornflake crumbs in a medium bowl.
Combine first set of ingredients. Mix well... (I use my Kitchen Aid mixer) Form into one (1) inch balls.
Roll meatballs in cornflake crumbs, slightly flatten, place in oil, brown quickly. Remove from skillet and arrange in two (2) qt baking dish. Combine mushroom soup and water. Pour over meatballs. Bake covered at 350 for 30min. Uncover and bake 20 min. longer.

Best served with mashed potatoes... (Idaho potatoes, of course!)

Connie Parish

Danielle's "Famous" Pork Chops
(only famous cause Scotty loves them)

Preheat oven to 375

Arrange pork chops in baking dish. Add a little bit of water so that it coats the bottom of the pan.
Sprinkle with seasoning, chopped onions, and brown sugar
Cover with catsup Bake for 1 hour

Danielle Keopke

Porko Chops

If you like moist golden fried pork chops – you'll love this simple recipe. Dan never liked pork chops till I converted him with this version. I like to use boneless chops – but you can use any type. Blend Panko bread crumbs (these are traditionally Japanese bread crumbs – made without the bread crust) and flour.

About 4 parts Panko to 1 part flour – add Lawry's Seasoned Salt. I recommend mixing it in a bag so you can shake the chops to evening coat them and clean up amounts to tossing the bag in the trash when done. Mix up an egg wash – dunk the chops in the egg and then into the bag.

Grill the chops over a medium heat – not too hot!! Cook slowly till they're a nice even light brown color.
You're welcome!

Cyd Peterson

Chicken Casserole

2 cups cooked chicken, chopped *See Below
1 cup chopped celery
1 can cream of chicken soup
1/2 cup mayo
1 tbs lemon juice
3 boiled eggs, chopped
Pepperidge Farm Stuffing mix
1/4 cup butter, melted

Preheat oven to 325.
Lightly grease a 6X6 casserole dish.
Mix all ingredients except Stuffing and butter.
Cover top with enough Pepperidge Farm to cover nicely.
Drizzle melted butter over top and bake for 30 minutes or bubbling nicely.

This recipe doubles nicely for a 9X 13, and I recommend it, as it is actually better left over.

* A couple of chicken breasts boiled will yield the two cups you need. I have also used
Pilgrim's pride chicken breast pieces with good results. They may need to be cut smaller.

Jim Davis

Loaded Chicken and Potatoes

Here's what you need:
1 lb boneless chicken breasts, cubed (1″) {glad you don't have to cube the bones}
6-8 medium red potatoes, cut in 1/2″ cubes (don't peel)
1/3 cup olive oil
1 1/2 tsp salt
1 tsp black pepper
1 Tbsp paprika
2 Tbsp garlic powder
2 Tbsp hot sauce – I use 1/4 cup diced green chili instead

Topping:
2 cups grated cheese – I use the Mexican blend
1 cup crumbled bacon
1 cup diced green onion

Preheat oven to 400 degrees and spray a 9 X 13″ baking dish with cooking spray. In a large bowl, mix the olive oil, salt, pepper, paprika, garlic powder, and hot sauce (or green chili) followed by the cubed potatoes and chicken. Stir it carefully to coat with the oil and seasonings. Transfer the coated potatoes and chicken into the baking dish.

Bake the potatoes and chicken for about an hour, stirring a few times. It should be browned on the outside, even a little crispy. During that time, fry your bacon until crispy, then let it drain so you can chop it up. When the potatoes and chicken are fully cooked, remove from the oven and top with the the cheese, bacon, and green onions. Return the pan to the oven and bake for about 5 minutes, until cheese is melted. Serve with some sour cream or ranch dressing. Add your favorite salad and/or some warm French bread.

Jeni Peterson

Loaded chicken and potatoes

1 lb. chicken breast, cubed
    {do we cube the bones for this recipe?}
    [I say always always cube the bones]
3 med. potatoes, 1/2 inch cubes
1/3 c. olive oil
salt and pepper
1T paprika
2 T garlic powder
2 T hot sauce

Mix all ingredients in large bowl. Pour into baking dish, bake @ 400
for 55 minutes
Top with 2 C shredded cheddar cheese
1 C bacon
1 C scallions

Bake until cheese is melted and bubbly

Karen Compton

Mexican Beef Triangles

1 sheet Edmonds butter puff pastry, thawed*
1 tablespoon milk
400 grams canned red kidney beans
1/2 red capsicum (approximately 60g/1/2 cup), diced
1 medium tomato (approximately 125g/3/4 cup), diced
salt and pepper
400 grams lean beef, cut into 1cm-wide strips
1 tablespoon olive oil
2 teaspoons chili powder
1/2 small iceberg lettuce, shredded
2 tablespoons sour cream
Instructions

1 Preheat oven to 200°C and line an oven tray with baking paper. Cut pastry sheet into 4 triangles and, using a butter knife, mark a 1cm border around each triangle, trying to avoid cutting all the way through. Brush pastry with milk and place on the baking tray. Bake for 12–15 minutes or until pastry is crisp and golden brown. Meanwhile, drain and rinse the kidney beans and place in a bowl with the capsicum and tomato. Season with salt and pepper, then set aside at room temperature until ready to serve.
Mix beef strips, oil and chili together. Heat a heavy-based frying pan over a high heat, add the beef and stir-fry until brown.
Place a pastry triangle on each plate. Divide lettuce and bean salsa evenly between each triangle and top with beef and a dollop of sour cream. Serves 4

Serve with grilled corn on the cob.

Tip: Squeeze lemon juice over each triangle and sprinkle with chopped coriander for extra flavour.
Preparation time: 20 minutes
Cooking time: 15 minutes

This recipe came to us via our friend Merv from Down Under. I was going to convert the measurements to US
But then I decided that if we just make it whilst standing on our heads and stir counter clockwise... we should be fine! Thanks again, Merv!

· A New Zealand product, not available in the US but Trader Joe's puts out a product called "Artisan Puff Pastry", which is made by Bay Bread Boulangerie in SF (though I believe this product is produced in a large commercial operation located elsewhere). It's an all-butter puff pastry (notoriously hard to find) and priced at $4.99 for two frozen sheets.

Rice and Bean Cakes

A recipe that I like to make a lot at once and freeze for lunches.
2 cups cooked rice
1 cup frozen corn kernels
1 cup pinto or black beans
⅔ cup grated cheddar cheese
2 green onions, trimmed and sliced (or use a regular onion, chopped)
2 eggs
½ tsp chili powder
½ tsp ground cumin
½ tsp salt
More Cheese!
you can also add ground hamburger, sausage, or turkey!

Preheat oven to 400 degrees.
I use my fancy Demarle medium cupcake pan to bake them in, but you can use a normal cupcake pan and spray it with cooking spray.
In a medium bowl, combine the rice, corn, beans, cheese and green onions. In a smaller bowl, whisk together the eggs, chili powder, cumin and salt. Add the egg mixture to the rice mixture and stir well.
Put mixture in the cupcake pan, top with cheese, and bake for 12-15 minutes. Let cool and enjoy!

Danielle Keopke

Dueling Pulled Pork!

My pulled pork is the best

Put a pork loin in a crockpot
Cover it with honey barbecue sauce
Cook on low for at least 6-8 hrs
When done shred with two forks while the meat is still in the crockpot

Sara Nageotte

No mine is!

Put a pork loin in a crockpot
Cover it with a can of Coke or root beer
Cook on low for at least 6-8 hours
When done shred with two forks while the meat is still in the crockpot

Tami Keenan

You decide which is the bestest!

Grandma's Noodles

Beat 8 eggs in a large bowl... Add enough flour to make dough... Make sure it's not too dry...

Put flour on the counter, knead dough on the counter till no longer sticky. {um, the dough or the counter?}
Cut dough in small sections.

Thin the dough using either a noodle pasta maker (dial on 3), or Kitchen aid noodle attachment. Cut noodles using either the pasta maker or Kitchen Aid attachment. {Connie, what if you don't have either of those thingies?????} {Is she ever gonna answer that one?} I hang them on a wooden clothes hanger that folds to dry. (crisp when broken).

The noodles may take a while to dry... In the summertime I take them outside and they dry real fast.

Take either a cut up chicken or chicken thighs, place in a large stockpot, add enough water to cover the chicken and a little more. (You want the fat for the juices) While it's cooking add salt and pepper. Cook till chicken is done. Pull chicken out and put on plate to keep warm. (Make sure you get all the bones out). Heat chicken juices, tasting to make sure you have enough salt and pepper. When juices are boiling turn down heat to medium, add noodles and stir... Cook over medium heat, stirring to make sure they don't burn on the bottom. Taste the noodles to check if they are done.

Best served with mashed potatoes...

Connie Parish

The One Pot Stop...

Soup

Bear Creek Solutions

Quick and tasty meals!

Bear Creek Creamy Potato Soup -
In a large soup pot, brown down (what if I want to brown up?)
Albertson's store brand spicy (yes... spicy) breakfast sausage; prepare
soup mix according to package, right on top of sausage. Peel and dice
an extra potato or two and add to the pot. Cook following directions
on package (Jeni just pilfered a batch I had frozen).

Bear Creek Minestrone –
Ina large soup pot, brown some Johnsonville spicy Italian sausage;
prepare soup mix according to package, right on top of sausage. Add
a can or two of petite diced tomatoes. (She took some of that as well!)

Bear Creek Cheddar Broccoli
Guess how this starts – prepare soup mix according to package – just
add some small chopped broccoli florets to make it heartier. Please
don't use frozen broccoli, you lazy bums!
Check out their other soups - I've made variations on many of them
for fast and DELISH meals.

Cyd Peterson

Beef Soup/Stew

Ingredients:

A big inexpensive chunk of steak (or if you have a lot of leftover steak, that works too!)

An onion

Montreal Steak Seasoning

Salt

Several cubes of beef bouillon

Several cans of diced tomatoes

A package of frozen mixed vegetables

A few potatoes

Instructions:

Dissolve 4 or 5 cubes of bouillon in 2 cups of water and set aside.

Cut the steak into small bite size pieces and brown it in a sauté pan {or sauté it in a brown pan works}, heavily sprinkle Montreal Steak Seasoning as it starts to brown {the meat or the seasoning turns brown?}, add onion and cook till the onion starts to look clear. Add the bouillon mix, bring to a boil and shut off the heat.

Transfer to a big stock pot and add diced tomatoes and mixed vegetables, let this simmer for an hour or longer. Peel and cube potatoes, add to the mixture, cook until potatoes are done.

Now get some good bread, sit your ass down and eat.

Cyd Peterson

Oven Stew

One big roast cut into (bite-size) stew size pieces
One large onion, quartered and cut once again
Couple big hands (please wash them first) full of carrots (I buy the
baby carrots)
5 or 6 or so potatoes cut into 1x1 pieces
1 large can tomato soup

Preheat oven to 375

Coat the stew meat in flour mixed with your favorite seasonings, (I
use Montreal steak seasoning, salt and pepper), brown in a big pot
that will soon go into the oven.
Throw in the onions, carrots, potatoes and tomato soup and mix
thoroughly.
Place the pot in the oven and cook for about 2 hours until the carrots
and potatoes are fork done.
When serving put a large spoon of sour cream on top.

So good on cold winter nights.

Nona Taft

Taco Soup

In a large pot;
1 - 2 lbs. ground beef
1 med. chopped onion

Cook together then drain off excess grease.

Add in;

1 package Hidden Valley Ranch dressing mix (Original...in the salad dressing aisle)
1 package taco seasoning

Add in all cans and do not drain off juices - they give the soup flavor and all the water it needs!

1 can Original Rotel Tomatoes and Green Chilies (found with canned tomatoes)
1 can red kidney beans (dark or light is fine)
1 can pinto beans
1 can whole kernel corn - same sized can {I'm confused, same sized can as what?} [the beans... dork]
1 can Campbell's beef broth

Simmer together for 30 minutes. Serve with Fritos and/or sour cream (optional) {as if you would eat this without either one}

Patty Deas

Chipotle Chicken Corn Chowder

Ingredients:

1 chipotle chile pepper in adobo sauce plus 1 teaspoon of the sauce (use only 1 chile - not 1 can)
2 tablespoons butter
1 poblano pepper, seeded and finely chopped
1 red bell pepper, seeded and finely chopped (yellow or orange pepper would be fine, too)
1 teaspoon ground cumin
½ teaspoon dried oregano
½ teaspoon dried thyme
6 garlic cloves, peeled and minced
2 tablespoons all-purpose flour
3 cups whole milk
2 cups chicken stock
6 small red potatoes, peeled and diced small
4 ounces Monterey Jack cheese, shredded (about 1 cup)
4 ounces Cheddar cheese, shredded (about 1 cup)
2 cups diced, cooked chicken
1 (30-ounce) can sweet corn, drained (frozen corn [thawed] would work - this is my preference)
1 (15-ounce) can cream-style corn
1 cup crushed tortilla chips (measured after crushing)
Juice from 1 lime (about 2 tablespoons)
Chopped cilantro or parsley, to garnish (optional)

Directions:

Remove one chile from the can of chiles and mince it. Remove 1 teaspoon of the adobo sauce and set it aside to be used later. You can save the remaining chiles and sauce for another use. (I freeze a pepper or two in snack-size plastic bags for single-serve portions when needed in the future.)

Melt the butter in a large Dutch oven or stock pot over medium heat. Add the poblano pepper, red bell pepper (I used a combination of red, yellow and orange), the chile from the can, cumin, thyme and oregano, and sauté for 5 to 7 minutes, or until the peppers become soft. Add the garlic, stir and cook for an additional 30 seconds, or until fragrant.

Stir in the flour with a wooden spoon {can we use a plastic spoon?} [NO plastic spoons or wire hangers] and cook for 1 minute, or until there is no longer any visible raw flour. Slowly stir in the milk and chicken broth, scraping up any bits from the bottom of the pan as you stir.Add the potatoes, bring the mixture to a boil, then reduce the heat to low and simmer for 10 to 15 minutes, or until the potatoes are tender and can be easily pierced with a knife.

Add the shredded cheeses a handful at a time, stirring after each addition until the cheese is completely melted.

Finally, stir in the chicken, all of the corn, the tortilla chips, lime juice and the reserved 1 teaspoon of adobo sauce (if you feel that the chowder is already spicy enough at this point, you can omit the adobo sauce or just use a lesser amount). Cover and cook for an additional 10 minutes, or until the soup is completely heated through.

Somebody pinned this, don't remember who – but WOW! It's the bomb diggity.

Cyd Peterson

Slow-Cooker Chicken Tortilla Soup

Ingredients: *be sure to check the Garnishments section!

1lb shredded chicken *I use 2 large breasts   1 (14.5oz) can of
chicken broth

1 (15oz) diced stewed tomatoes   10oz frozen corn

1 (10oz) can enchilada sauce   1 med. onion, chopped

1 can black beans (I rinse mine 1st)   1 yellow pepper,
chopped

1 (4oz) can chopped green chile peppers   1 lime

2 (or more!) minced garlic cloves

Spices:

1 tsp cumin *I use 2 heaping tsp   big handful cilantro,
chopped

1 tsp chili powder *I use 2 heaping tsp   red pepper flakes

1 tsp black pepper *I eyeball it   oregano

1 bay leaf *I use 5   paprika (1 tsp, roughly)

Salt (sea, garlic, table...your call)

Directions:

Alright folks, here's the deal. This recipe is a modification of one that I found, but have made into my own. Apparently I like more flavor than most J So as for all of the spices, use your judgment based on your own preferences. I also like my soups to be thicker, more like stew, so I don't add any water to this, even though the original recipe calls for it.

1. Get out your crock pot
2. Open all the cans of stuff & dump 'em in. (tomatoes, enchilada sauce, green chile peppers, black beans)
3. Toss in: chopped onion, chopped yellow pepper, chopped cilantro, juice of lime, garlic- give it a quick stir
4. Add frozen corn (I use sweet white, & eyeball it)
5. Add spices: cumin, chili powder, black pepper, salt, cilantro, red pepper flakes, oregano, paprika

6. At this point, the only thing missing is the chicken broth & the chicken. I add the amount of chicken broth that mostly fills my medium sized crock pot. Stir it all together. As for the chicken, I toss my breasts in (sometimes frozen even!) raw. If you choose to do this, you will have to pull the breasts out 1hr-30 mins before you're ready to serve it, shred them, then toss the now shredded chicken back in and stir it. I do it this way because I'm lazy. If you'd prefer to cook & shred your chicken in place of step 1, by all means!

7. Cook high 4 hrs, low 6 hrs. The beauty of this recipe & the crock pot is that it's pretty much fool-proof. I have never OVER cooked it.

Garnishments:

These are all optional. But in my opinion, these MAKE the soup:

    -sprinkle with shredded cheese

    -add a dollop of sour cream

    -add fresh chopped cilantro

    -squeeze fresh lime juice over top

    -some chopped fresh avocado

    -a few crunched up tortilla chips

Enjoy!

Brett Ockerman

Creamy Swiss Cheese & Broccoli Soup

1 C. chopped ham
1 C. water
1 10oz frozen chopped broccoli
2 C milk
3 T flour
2 C. (8oz) swiss cheese (cubed)
½ tsp salt
Dash pepper

Boil ham in water for 10 min; add broccoli. Cook til tender. In a separate bowl gradually add milk to flour. Mix well. Mix with ham and broccoli till well blended. Stir till mixture gradually thickens. Simmer 5 minutes. Let cool down a little (if you don't let it cool down the cheese will curdle). Add cheese and seasoning. Cook till cheese is melted.

Connie Parish

Corn Chowder

½ pound of thick cut bacon, cut into stripes
5 medium potatoes, peeled and cubes
4 cups chicken broth
2 cans cream style corn
1 can regular corn
1 tsp dried thyme
½ tsp pepper
2 cups milk
Salt to taste

Slowly fry up bacon in heavy bottomed pot, making sure to render out as much fat as possible.
Remove bacon (leaving fat in pot) and set aside on a paper towel lined plate.
Add potatoes, chicken broth, thyme, and pepper to pot. Stir well, then cover and simmer for about 30 minutes, or until potatoes are tender.
Add in the corn, cream corn, and milk, stir well, then cook until heated thoroughly.
Pour into bowls and top with bacon, then eat.
Makes about 3 quarts

Victoria Taft

Chili

Already a hottly contested category - this year we have a new submission by a new submitter. I often don't have time to try a new recipe before putting the book together but dayum, this looked so good I had to try it. I gotta say - all you bitches pack up your spices and go home - Geoff now owns this category!

El Cid Chili

Ingredients

2 tablespoons olive oil
2 pounds sirloin steak, cut into 1-inch cubes
1/2 pound ground beef
12 ounces chorizo sausage, casing removed, cut into 1/2 cubes
1 large yellow onion, coarsely chopped
1/4 cup chili powder
1 tablespoon garlic salt
2 teaspoons cumin
1 teaspoon dried basil
2 (14.5-ounce) cans beef broth
2 (14.5-ounce) cans whole tomatoes, drained
1 cup cilantro, chopped
1 cinnamon stick
3 bay leaves
2 green jalapenos, slit lengthwise 3 times each
1 tablespoon yellow cornmeal
Salt and pepper, to taste
Garnish with Cheddar and sour cream, if desired.

Directions

Place oil in a large, heavy pot over medium heat. Brown the sirloin in batches. Remove to a bowl with a slotted spoon. Add ground beef, chorizo and onions to the pot and brown. Make sure to break up the meat. Return sirloin to the pot. Stir in remaining ingredients, except for garnishes. Bring to a boil, reduce heat, simmer for 2 hours. Stir occasionally, breaking up tomatoes. Before serving, discard cinnamon stick, bay leaves and jalapenos. Garnish, if desired.

The recipes for this program, which were provided by contributors and guests who may not be professional chefs, have not been tested in the Food Network's kitchens. Therefore, the Food Network cannot attest to the accuracy of any of the recipes.
(Geoff's Note) : You can add a couple of cans of kidney beans for more volume without really hurting the chili, if you're looking for a cheap way to feed a bunch of people.

Total Time: 3 hr
Prep: 30 min
Cook: 2 hr 30 min

Yield:8 servings

Geoff Gunkler

My Chili

2 lbs red beans
3 to 4 lb roast (venison is good)
Chili powder to taste
Diced mators (as much or as little as you see fit)
Sweet peppers (6 or so small ones)
Tomato sauce (add enough to make it as runny or thick as you want.
Big farking Walla Walla onion
Peanut butter (yes, I said peanut butter)

Soak your beans overnight. Rinse 'em off and add clean water to cover them plus a couple inches. Cook them under tender. Strain and set aside. Cut the roast into small bite size pieces and brown them with a bit of oil in a big pot (big enough to add the beans and everything else) while the meat is browning add the onions and peppers to it. At this point I add a little Monterey Steak seasoning cuz it is killer good. Once the meat and onions and peppers are cooked add your tomato sauce and chili powder to taste. I don't care for hot chili. If you want it hotter add more chili powder and/ or jalapeños (yuck). Once you have your sauce to taste add the beans and about half a cup of peanut butter and let it simmer for a bit. At this point you can add more tomato sauce if it seems too thick. About half an hour before eating add a couple small cans of diced tomatoes.

Nona Taft

Kick Cyd's Butt Chili

(I make spaghetti sauce too, but I can't beat hers – I won't admit that in very many areas. I also have thicker hair than she does though.) [Editor's Note: she's been cooking for 2½ years and already thinks she's a pro!] (and I'm the nice one too)

Start with a chopped onion and chopped yellow pepper. Sauté them a while in some butter while you brown the ground beef. Drain most of the grease off the meat, but you'll want just a little for flavor. Mix those together and cook for a while and season it with salt, pepper, seasoning salt, garlic powder, crushed red pepper, and some Mrs. Dash. Throw it in the slow cooker with a couple cans of chopped tomatoes, a can of tomato sauce, and a half can of water (more if you want it juicer), a can each of dark and light kidney beans not drained. Add at least one envelope of chili seasoning and as much chili powder as you want (if you want it hotter add some crushed red pepper flakes) and let it simmer for a couple hours.

Tami Keenan

3 Bean Chili

6 strips of bacon
1-2 lbs of ground beef
1 large onion
1 (16oz) can kidney beans
1 (16oz) can pinto beans
2 cans pork 'n beans
1 regular bottle of chili sauce
½ cup brown sugar

Dice and fry bacon till crisp. Drain.
Brown beef and onions drain, if necessary.
Combine all ingredients in a Crockpot and cook on medium till hot, or bake 1 hour uncovered at 350.

Connie Parish

Chili con Carne

1 lb ground beef (or turkey)
1 small-medium onion finely chopped
1-2 cloves of garlic
1 red bell pepper, chopped (or more!)
saute above until meat is browned and onions are transparent
Then add (approximately - feel free to mess with the amounts of the spices!):
1 tsp oregano
1 tsp cumin
1-2 T. chili powder (start on the low end and work up)
couple shakes of cinnamon (this is the "secret" ingredient - - - and I think it takes it up a notch!)
Add some broth (chicken, beef, veggie - whatever you have on hand) - about 1/2 - 1 cup
Add some tomato paste (around 2-3oz)
Add one can each of red kidney beans and white kidney beans (Cannellini)
Add more broth if you think it seems too thick

Let it simmer about 30 minutes on the stove, or longer if using the crock pot!

Lexis Hamilton

Side Dishes...

Drop Dumplings

1 ½ cups all-purpose flour
3 ½ teaspoons baking powder
½ teaspoon salt
¾ cup milk
Chopped parsley, if desired

Mix all dry ingredients thoroughly and add milk all at once, stir with a fork rapidly until well blended. If you're adding parsley, do it now. Drop by teaspoonfuls on top of whatever stewed meat and/veggies you've prepared. Dipping the spoon into the hot broth each time before dipping into the batter will prevent it from sticking to the spoon. When they are all in, cover and boil moderately for 12 minutes WITHOUT uncovering. Should yield about 5 servings.

Cyd Peterson

Grandpa's Corn

Ingredients:

6 eggs
2 sleeves of saltine crackers
2 cups milk
1 cup shredded cheese
10 dollops Crisco {how much is a dollop anyway?}
3 cans creamed corn

Instructions:
Crush saltines, set ½ aside, mix all other ingredients except Crisco.
Pour into a 9 x 13 glass pan, sprinkle with the remaining crushed
saltine and plop the dollops of Crisco around on the top.

{I'm sure this is entirely healthy for your arteries}

Bake at 350 till firm – prolly around an hour.

Sounds weird…. Tastes great!

Dan Peterson

Oven-Baked Zucchini Parmesan Crisps

2 medium zucchini
1/4 teaspoon salt
1/2 teaspoon freshly ground pepper
1/2 teaspoon garlic powder
1 tablespoon olive oil
1 large egg white
1/2 cup panko bread crumbs
1/2 cup coarsely grated Parmesan cheese

Preheat the oven to 450°F and lightly grease a baking sheet with olive oil.

Slice the zucchini into 1/4 inch rounds. Put the zucchini coins in a bowl and season with salt, pepper, and garlic powder. Mix in the olive oil and the egg toss to coat evenly.

Mix the panko crumbs and Parmesan together in a small bowl. Working with a few slices at a time, put the zucchini in the panko Parmesan mixture and place on the greased baking sheet.

Bake for 25 minutes, or until the zucchini are brown and crispy.

Nona Taft

Corn Squashy Stuff

Ingredients:

Butternut squash
Frozen corn
(However much you want, but try to make it 2 parts squash/1 part
corn. Nnnnkay?)
Butter
Eagle Brand (sweetened) milk

Instructions:

Heat and/or cook squash and mash it smooth, similar to mashed
potato consistency. Rinse frozen corn with hot water, drain well and
mix with squash – don't pulverize the corn! Add butter and Eagle milk
until the mixture is a little soupy and tastes kinda sweet. I usually
nuke it for 5 minutes and then bake it for 20 – 30, until the very top is
a little crunchy.

And POOF, this is how they serve squash and corn in Puerto Vallarta.
OLE! Right Jim?

Cyd Peterson

Sweet Potato Shuffle

Ingredients:
2 cans yams
1 egg
½ cup milk
½ stick margarine
½ cup crushed nuts
½ cup brown sugar
1 tsp cinnamon
Handful of marshmallows (the small ones) {please wash your hands}
[what, like we're all unsanitary people – sheesh!]
½ cup raisins

Instructions:
Preheat oven to 350
Blend yams, egg, milk and margarine. Stir in the handful of
marshmallows and raisins. Pour into an oiled 9 x 13 baking pan. Mix
the nuts, brown sugar and cinnamon and spread of the top.
Bake until hot – about 30 minutes.

Cyd Peterson

Green Beans

Fry up 4- 5 slices of bacon till crisp. Save the grease... crumple {is that the same thing as crumble?} up the bacon
Put in a crock pot:
2 cans cut green beans
½ cup chopped onions
Fill the Crockpot with water almost to the top..
Add some salt, pepper, little bit of sugar (or splenda), the bacon and grease...
Cook all day...

Jeni Peterson

It's Really Keen(an) Mac & Cheese

As much Velveeta as you want, but at least half of the big block
½ block of Pepper Jack cheese
1 can of Pet milk
Cooked macaroni
Salt and pepper to taste
A little butter won't hurt.
Mix it all together and bake it for at least 30 minutes, sprinkle with bread crumbs or crushed cracker. If it's too thick add a little milk.

Tami Keenan

Fancy Pants" Bacon Mac 'n Cheese

4 strips regular bacon and 4 strips of pepper bacon, diced into ½ inch pieces
1 clove garlic, chopped
6 oz heavy cream
4 oz chicken broth
8 oz shredded cheddar cheese
2 oz shredded Parmesan cheese
½ teaspoon black pepper
8 oz (uncooked weight) noodle of your choice – we like penne
½ cup seasoned, dried breadcrumbs
Set oven to 350.
Cook pasta to al dente, drain and set aside, while that is cooking, cook the bacon until almost crisp in a medium oven-proof skillet. Add the garlic and allow to soften in the bacon fat. Add the cream, bring to a boil, add the cheeses and drained pasta, top with the seasoned bread crumbs and put into the oven until lightly browned and bubbling. Yeah, uh huh... it's how we roll. {this stuff is soooo good!}

Dan Peterson

Noodle Rice Casserole

1/2 lb. margarine melted in large pan
1/2 lb. fine egg noodles, brown in margarine
2 C. instant rice, add to noodles
2 cans chicken broth, pour into mixture
2 cans onion soup, pour into mixture
1 can water, add a little soy sauce
Put all into baking dish, cook @ 350 for about 25-30 minutes

Karen Compton

Breads and carbfulls...

Lemon Zucchini Bread

2 cups cake flour
½ teaspoon. salt
2 teaspoon baking powder
2 eggs
½ cup canola oil
1⅓ cups sugar
2 tablespoons lemon juice
½ cup buttermilk
zest of 1 lemon
1 cup grated zucchini

Glaze
1 cup powdered sugar
2 tablespoon lemon juice
1 tablespoon milk

Mix flour, salt and baking powder in a medium bowl and set aside.
In a large bowl, beat eggs. Then add oil and sugar until well blended.
Add lemon juice, buttermilk, lemon zest to this mixture and blend all
together.
Fold in zucchini until it is mixed well.
Add dry mixture to the wet mixture and blend all together until well
combined.
Pour batter into greased 9x5 loaf pan.
Bake at 350 for 40-45 minutes.
While still warm, make glaze and spoon over the bread. Let the glaze
set up before cutting and serving

Nona Taft

Patty's Rolls

Ingredients:
6 to 6 1/2 cups all-purpose flour
½ cup sugar
2 teaspoons salt
2 packages active dry yeast
1 cup butter or margarine, softened
1 egg

Instructions:
About 3 1/2 hours before serving:
In a large bowl combine 2 ¼ cups flour, sugar, salt and yeast; add ½ cup
butter. With mixer at low speed, gradually pour 2 cups hot tap water
(120° to 130° F) into dry ingredients. Add egg; increase speed to
medium; beat 2 minutes, occasionally scraping bowl with rubber
spatula. Beat in ¾ cup flour or enough to make a thick batter continue
beating 2 minutes, occasionally scraping the bowl. With a wooden
spoon; stir in enough additional flour (about 2 ½ cups), to make a soft
dough.
Turn dough onto lightly floured surface and knead until smooth and
elastic, about 10 minutes. Shape dough into a ball and place in greased
large bowl, turning over so that top of dough is greased. Cover with
towel, let rise in warm (happy) place (80° to 85° F.) until doubled, about
1 ½ hours.
Punch down dough by pushing down the center of dough with fist,
then pushing edges of dough to center. Turn dough onto lightly floured
surface; knead lightly to make smooth ball; cover with bowl for 15
minutes and let dough rest.

In 17 ¼" by 11 ½" roasting pan (or baking sheet), over low heat, melt remaining ½ cup butter; tilt pan to grease bottom.
On lightly floured surface with floured rolling pin, roll dough ½ inch thick. With floured 2 ¾" round cutter (I have also used a clean soup can with holes cut in the bottom), cut dough into circles. Holding dough circle by the edge, dip both sides into melted butter pan, fold in half. Arrange folded dough in rows in pan, each nearly touching the other. Knead trimmings together, roll and cut more rolls. Cover pan with towel; let dough rise in warm place until doubled, about 40 minutes.
Meanwhile, preheat oven to 425° F. Bake rolls 18 to 20 minutes until browned. Makes about 3 ½ dozen.

Patty Deas

Tortillas

3 cups flour
1/2 cup Crisco
1 tsp baking powder
1 tsp salt
2 cups warm water

Instructions:
Mix all the ingredients together, but add the warm water gradually, you don't want it to stick.
Let it stand 15 – 30 minutes.
Roll balls of dough, depending on the size you want and flatten in your hand.
Roll on floured surface making them 1/8" thick.
Cook on griddle at a medium heat until light spots appear, then flip.

Lynn Compton

Yogurt Zucchini Bread

2 Cups flour
½ t baking powder
½ t baking soda
¾ Cups plus 2 T sugar
2 Large eggs
½ Cup veggie oil
½ Cup fat free plain Greek Yogurt
1 Cup coarsely grated zucchini

Whisk the flour with the other dry ingredients except the sugar. In another bowl mix the sugar with the wet ingredients 'cepting the zucchini. Add the wet stuff to the dry stuff and mix well then add the zucchini. Grease a 9x4 ½ loaf pan and bake at 325 for about an hour or so. If you toast your nuts (Wally nuts) they are good in it tew.
Out of desperation, cuz my husband thinks it's neat to plant numerous zucchini plants; we had the little buggers coming out our ears. This recipe gives a little twist to the mundane zucchini bread and makes it a little moister.

[my spidey sense tells me Zucchini is plentiful at the Taft residence]

Nona Taft

'Nanner Bread

No one in our house doesn't love the banana bread muffins we make using this recipe.

2 cups all-purpose flour
3/4 cup sugar
1/2 cup vegetable oil
1 egg
1/2 teaspoon salt
1 teaspoon baking soda
3 ripe bananas
1/2 teaspoon vanilla

Optional: 1/4 cup walnuts and/or a pinch of cinnamon

Preheat oven to 350. Mix sugar, oil and eggs until creamy. Add bananas and nuts(if desired) and then mix some more. Add all other ingredients and mix until smooth. Put in a muffin tin and bake until toothpick comes out clean. We have found this to be about 25 minutes. [you scienced it?!]

Lexis Hamilton

Nageotte Rhymes with Gadget Cheesy Bread

Loaf of French bread, sliced length-wise, with the center removed
Mayonnaise
Chopped green onion
Shredded cheese
Mix the last three as much as you want of each and fill up the hollowed center of the loaf of bread and close it back up. Wrap it in foil and bake @350 for about 20 minutes . Let it stand a little while before you slice it or all the guts will ooze out.

Tami Keenan who stole it from Sarah Nageotte

Condiments...

Fresh Salsa

Ingredients:

A slew of Roma tomatoes
Fresh garlic
One lime
One sweet onion
A couple of Anaheim peppers (not Los Angeles)
A jalapeño pepper (not on a stick)
One can black beans

Instructions:
Chop tomatoes into very small chunks, you can try a food processor, but I always found that they tend to pulverize the tomatoes too much. So be prepared... this takes awhile. Chop up the onion and peppers; be sure to remove the seeds. Smash and chop fine 3 large cloves of garlic – careful here; a little goes a long way. Add in the can of black beans; season the entire mixture with a little salt. Squeeze lime juice, depending on how many tomatoes you use – start with ¼ of the lime for a small batch, up the entire lime for a large batch. Stir it well and let it get happy – prolly 45 minutes or so. Then and ONLY then, taste test for spices, add more as needed. If you've put too much of something, well then... you're screwed.
Serve with tortilla chips and apply with tequila.

Cyd Peterson

Desserts...

Strawberry Cream Cheese Cobbler

1 stick butter
1 egg lightly beaten
1 cup milk
1 cup all-purpose flour
1 cup sugar
2 teaspoons baking powder
1/2 teaspoon salt
2 quarts strawberries capped and washed
4 ounces cream cheese cut in small pieces

Preparation
Preheat oven to 350 degrees. Melt butter and pour into 9x13 glass baking dish. In a small bowl, mix together the egg, milk, flour, sugar, baking powder, and salt. Pour directly over the butter in the baking dish, but do not stir.
Add the strawberries, arranging in a single layer as much as possible. Sprinkle cream cheese pieces over strawberries. Place in preheated oven and bake 45 minutes, or until top is golden brown and edges are bubbling. (Crust rises up and around the fruit, but fruit will still peek out of top.) [Oh my!]

Karen Compton

Galveston, oh... GalVESTONNNNNNN

Ingredients:
1 stick of margarine
2 cups flour
1 cup chopped pecans
1 8 oz package of softened cream cheese
1 cup powdered sugar
1 cup Cool Whip
1 4 ½ oz instant chocolate pudding
1 4 ½ oz instant vanilla pudding
2 cups milk

Instructions:
Preheat oven to 350, blend and spread into a 9 x 13 baking pan – 1 stick of margarine, 1 cup flour and 1 cup pecans. Bake 20 – 30 minutes and cool.
Mix cream cheese, powdered sugar and Cool Whip – spread onto cooled crust.
Mix chocolate and vanilla pudding with milk, layer on top of cream cheese layer – do this part fast, the pudding sets up quickly.
Top with Cool Whip and let it chillax for a bit. {I stole her recipe for a Decadent Dessert Day at work once and won the award!}

Cyd Peterson

Treebird's Buttercake

Preheat oven to 350°

There is nothing quite as decadent as this buttercake. The buttery crust is topped with a rich cream cheese layer.

CRUST
3 cups Pillsbury Plus yellow cake mix*
1/2 cup butter or margarine, melted
1 egg

FILLING
3 1/3 cups powdered sugar, sifted
2 eggs
2 teaspoons vanilla
3 3-ounce packages cream cheese, softened
1 1/2 cups powdered sugar, sifted

* Each box of cake mix yields 3 cups dry mix.

FOR CRUST:
Generously spray a 10 x 15-inch jelly roll pan with non-stick spray. With an electric mixer, blend dry cake mix, melted butter and 1 egg on low speed until moist. Pat onto bottom and sides of prepared pan. Set aside.

FOR FILLING:
With electric mixer on low speed mix 3 1/3 cups sifted powdered sugar, 2 eggs, vanilla and cream cheese until ingredients are moistened. Turn mixer to high speed and beat for 5 minutes. Turn mixer to low speed. Add remaining 1 1/2 cups sifted powdered sugar and mix until well blended. Return mixer to high speed; beat for 5 minutes. Pour mixture over crust in pan and spread evenly.

Bake at 350° for 40 minutes, or until golden brown. When cool, slice into squares.

You need to make sure you are close to a hospital when you go into a diabetic coma.

Patty Deas

Damn Good Pumpkin Pie

Ingredients:
One 9 inch unbaked pastry shell
1 16 oz can of pumpkin – srsly... only Libbeys.
One 14 oz can of eagle milk – Buzzard milk will not work!
2 eggs
1 teaspoon ground cinnamon
½ teaspoon ground ginger ½ teaspoon ground nutmeg
½ teaspoon salt
Instructions:
Preheat oven to 425. In large bowl combine all ingredients except for the pastry shell (did I really need to point that out?), mix well and pour into shell.

Bake 15 minutes. Reduce heat to 350 and continue baking 35 – 40 minutes or until a toothpick in the middle comes out clean. The pie will firm up a little more once removed from the oven.
Cool it, eat it, love it

Cyd Peteron

One Cup

Ingredients:
1 cup flour
1 cup milk
1 cup sugar
½ stick butter

Cream together and pour over any sort of fruit/fruit filling, bake at 375 for 45 minutes and presto-chango – it's cobbler.

Cyd Peterson

Waldorf Astoria Cake

Ingredients:
3 Tablespoons of Nestles Quick
2 oz bottle of red food color
½ cup shortening – something like Crisco
1 ½ cup sugar
2 eggs
1 cup buttermilk
2 ¼ cups floor
1 Tablespoon of vanilla
A dash of salt
1 Tablespoon of vinegar
1 teaspoon of baking soda
Instructions:
Mix the Nestles and food color, set aside and let stand
Cream together the shortening, sugar and eggs. Blend in dye mixture,
buttermilk, flour, vanilla and dash of salt. In a separate bowl, mix the
vinegar and baking soda... watch it react... cool huh? {Hey, Cyd,
remember when we used to mix vinegar and baking soda in Mom's old
pill bottles and wait for the tops to blow off and Mom would get mad at
us because we put marks on the ceiling? That was sooo cool!} Now mix
it into the batter.
Pour into 2 greased round 9" cake pans, or 3 8" cake pans, or 4 7' cake
pans, or 5 6" cake pans, or... Bake at 350 for 30 – 35 minutes or until a
toothpick comes clean out of the middle. Don't make loud noises or jar
the oven – this scratch cake will fall, it's excited!
Once it's done, let it cool – pop it out of the pan, frost with cream cheese
frosting.

You'll sometimes see variations of this recipe and it's referred to as Red
Velvet Cake. But this specific recipe is from the Waldorf Astoria Hotel
in New York. At one time it was one of the most sought after recipes in
the country, second only to the Neiman Marcus cookie recipe. Both
were the best kept secret recipes in the country.

Cyd Peterson

Heidi's Grandma's Carrot Cake

I got this is recipe from an old co-worker after I told her I'd never had carrrot cake and it sounded disgusting. She proved me wrong. This cake is moist and delicious. Plus it will keep you regular.

3 cups all-purpose flour
1 1/2 cups canola oil
2 teaspoons baking soda
16 ounces crushed pineapple with juice
1 teaspoon salt
2 cups grated carrots
3 eggs
2 teaspoons vanilla
2 cups sugar

Sift dry ingredients together and then add others. Mix well. Bake at 350 for 45-min to an hour. Check with toothpick. Pairs well with homemade cream cheese frosting. (That is the only kind of frosting for carrot cake)

Homemade Cream Cheese Frosting

Another recipe from Heidi's Grandma. You'll want to make two batches at once, at least, depending on what you're using the frosting for.

1 stick butter
1 8 ounce package of cream cheese (Philadelphia, of course)
1 pound powdered sugar
2 teaspoons vanilla
1/2 teaspoon salt

In a mixer, cream the butter with the cream cheese. Add powdered sugar and other ingredients. Then beat on high until smooth and creamy (feel free to check for texture by tasting...) [I wouldn't dream of not tasting this mixture!] Use liberally on baked goods. Unless you're counting calories. Then avoid this at all costs. [A great candidate for the Waldorf Astoria cake!]

Lexis Hamilton

Cinnamon Roll Cake

Cake:
3 C Flour
¼ Tsp. Salt
1 C. Sugar
1 ½ C milk
2 eggs
2 Tsp Vanilla
½ C butter melted

Topping:
1 C butter, softened
1 C brown Sugar
2 Tbsp Flour
1 Tbsp cinnamon

Mix everything together except for the butter. Slowly stir in the melted butter and pour into a greased 9x13 pan. For the topping, mix all the ingredients together until well combined and drop evenly over the batter and swirl with a knife. Bake at 350 for around 30 or 35 minutes.

Glaze:
2 C powdered sugar
5 Tbsp milk
1 Tsp Vanilla

While the cake is still warm drizzle the glaze over the cake
This cake actually taste likes a cinnamon roll and will put you into a diabetic coma if you eat too much. [I make that 2 diabetic coma recipes in this section alone!]

Nona Taft

Snackage...

Almond Roca

1 cup butter
1 ½ cup firmly packed brown sugar
1 12oz pkg. chocolate chips
4 cups or more of chopped almonds

Spread some chopped almonds (2 cups?) in an edged cookie sheet. Melt butter in cast iron skillet. Add brown sugar. Cook over medium heat. When comes to a boil cook for 10 minutes more. Stir constantly. Pour HOT candy mixture over almonds. Add chocolate chips. Spread chips when melted. Sprinkle the rest of the almonds on top of melted chips. Cool and break into pieces... Enjoy... {I'm going to try this when I get my permanent crowns in}

Connie Parish

Connie's Carmel Corn

Preheat oven to 250

2 sticks of butter
2 cups brown sugar
½ cup Karo Light corn syrup
½ tsp. vanilla
½ tsp. baking soda
2 packages Chester's Puff corn, butter flavored

Place puffcorn in a large roasting pan and set aside. In a large saucepan, combine butter, sugar and corn syrup. Cook over medium heat. When comes to a boil time for 5 min. Stirring occasionally. After 5 minutes, stir in vanilla and baking soda. It will bubble up. Pour over Puff corn and mix well. Bake for 1 hour, stir it every 15 minutes.

Connie Parish

75

Pepper Cookies (AKA Snicker Doodles)

Preheat oven to 350

1 cup butter
1 ½ cup sugar
2 Eggs

Beat those together thoughly

In another bowl combine:
2 ¾ C flour
2 tsp. Cream of tartar
1 tsp. Baking soda
¼ tsp. salt

Combine some sugar and cinnamon in a medium bowl.

Take mixture and make tsp. size balls, put in sugar/cinnamon
mixture, coat well.

Place on cookie sheet lined with parchment paper. Bake for 10 min.
They will be doughy when you pull them out. Cool and enjoy

Connie Parish

Super soft yummy SuGaR CoOkIEs

Sift
3 C flour
1 t baking powder
1 t salt

Blend
1.5 C sugar
1 C butter (unsalted)
1 t Vanilla
3 Eggs unbeaten

Add dry ingredients to the sugar mixture. Pour out gooey mixture on a floured surface. Put a little flour on top and roll out to about half an inch think. Cut with whatever you want in your favorite edible shapes or whatever. Bake at 375 about 11 minutes or so or until edges start to brown.

Nona Taft

P-ness Buttered Balls

1 Lb unsalted butter
1 lb peanut butter
2 lb powdered sugar
3 t Vanilla
24 oz chocolate chips
1.5 sq bakers wax

Melt butter and add peanut butter till smooth . Add vanilla and sugar until smooth. Roll into 1 inch balls. Place on cookie sheet covered in wax paper. Put a toothpick in each one. Place in fridge for about 3 hours.

Melt chocolate and wax. Dip your balls in the wax and set them on another cookie sheet covered in wax paper. Place them back in the fridge for another hour or so until set. Makes about 150 balls. – Don't forget to give a dozen or so to Cyd, really... don't just talk about doing it, do it!

Nona Taft

Rules to Cook by and Other Ridiculous Stuff...

Gravy Mixes – Use ONLY Knorr - that being said:

How to make gravy from scratch.

All gravy starts the same way – with a roux.
Short list for ingredients and yields:
1 tablespoon of flour and 1 tablespoon of butter for each cup of liquid.
Allow butter to melt slowly over a medium heat – add the flour and
stir well. Make sure the butter and flour are completely blended,
allow it to cook a little till it bubbles a bit and turns golden. The more
it browns the less it will thicken your gravy or sauce and be careful
not to scorch it. Add the liquid and stir constantly – a whisk is very
helpful here. Allow it to cook a little to thicken – remember that it
will continue to thicken after it's taken off the heat.
For gravies just add whatever stock you have. You can use the same
roux and add milk for a white sauce.
Roux is super easy and the key to pretty much any kind of gravy or
white sauce. Have a caution when you're making it – flour heats up
very hot and maintains a high temp for a long time – if it splashes out
of the pan you'll get a nasty burn. Just pay attention to what you're
doing. Nnnnkay?

Always use Lawry's Seasoned Salt on pork.

You can never have enough cheese

Panko – Panko - Panko

Obviously if you're going to make the recipes in this book you need clean hands or hand sanitizer. Rubber gloves would work, but that's probably a subject for a whole nother book.

Vidalia Onions – BAM!

Ever wonder how long you can freeze stuff?

Here's some answers:

Pork Chops – 4 – 6 months
Steaks – 6 – 12 months
Ground Beef – 3 – 4 months
Bacon – 1 month
Sausage 1 – 2 months
Chicken (cut up) 9 months
Lobster 12 months
Crab 10 months
Shrimp 3 – 6 months

... slightly off topic, but here's some tres cool cleaning hacks:

Tub Cleaner - vinegar and dish soap, no scrubbing! Heat 1/2C white vinegar in m'wave for 90 sec, pour into spray bottle. Add 1/2 Cup BLUE Dawn dish soap. Shake gently to mix. Spray on surface, let it sit 1-2 hours. Just wipe it away then rinse with water. Should also take soap scum off shower doors!

Dust your ceiling fan blades with a pillowcase – when you're done take it outside, turn the case wrong side out and shake all the dust out.

Use old dryer sheets to wipe down baseboards. And because they're anti static they'll stay dust free longer.

WD40 will remove crayon marks from LCD screens.

If you're out of fabric softener or dryer sheets, you can crumple up aluminum foil into balls and throw into the dryer to eliminate static cling.